The Tough Task

Craig Wright

T0352695

Name _____

Age _____

Class _____

OXFORD
UNIVERSITY PRESS

OXFORD
UNIVERSITY PRESS

Great Clarendon Street, Oxford OX2 6DP

Oxford University Press is a department of the University of Oxford.
It furthers the University's objective of excellence in research, scholarship,
and education by publishing worldwide in

Oxford New York

Auckland Cape Town Dar es Salaam Hong Kong Karachi
Kuala Lumpur Madrid Melbourne Mexico City Nairobi
New Delhi Shanghai Taipei Toronto

With offices in

Argentina Austria Brazil Chile Czech Republic France Greece
Guatemala Hungary Italy Japan South Korea Poland Portugal
Singapore Switzerland Thailand Turkey Ukraine Vietnam

OXFORD and OXFORD ENGLISH are registered trade marks of
Oxford University Press in the UK and in certain other countries

ISBN-13: 978 0 19 440107 4
ISBN-10: 0 19 440107 3

Printed in China

Illustrations by: Sarah Kuo

With thanks to Sally Spray for her contribution to this series

To my Dad, Ernest, and my Mom, Lynn

Using the book

1 Begin by looking at the first story page (page 2). Look at the picture and ask questions about it. Then read the story text under the picture with your students. **Use section 1 of the CD for this if possible.**

2 Teach and check the understanding of any new vocabulary. Note that some of the words are in the **Picture Dictionary** at the back of the book.

3 Now look at the activities on the right-hand page. Show the example to the students and instruct them to complete the activities. This may be done individually, in pairs, or as a class.

4 Do the same for the remaining pages of the book.

5 Retell the whole story more quickly, reinforcing the new vocabulary. **Section 2 of the CD can help with this.**

6 **If possible, listen to the expanded story (section 3 of the CD). The students should follow in their books.**

7 When the book is finished, use the **Picture Dictionary** to check that students understand and remember new vocabulary. **Section 4 of the CD can help with this.**

Using the CD

The CD contains four sections.

1 The story told slowly, with pauses. Use this during the first reading. It may also be used for "Listen and repeat" activities at any point.

2 The story told at normal speed. This should be used once the students have read the book for the first time.

3 The expanded story. The story is told in a longer version. This will help the students understand English when it is spoken faster, as they will now know the story and the vocabulary.

4 Vocabulary. Each word in the **Picture Dictionary** is spoken and then used in a simple sentence.

Lee Ming is an old grandfather. He lives in China with his family.

He is at home with his grandchildren. He is telling a story. The story is about a tough task.

1 Check ✓ true or false.

	True	False
❶ They are at the park.	☐	✓
❷ Lee Ming is Chinese.	☐	☐
❸ The grandchildren are listening to a story.	☐	☐
❹ They live in China.	☐	☐
❺ Lee Ming has two grandsons.	☐	☐

2 Complete.

❶ Lee Ming is an ___old___ man.

❷ He has _____ grandchildren.

❸ He is telling a _____ .

❹ His _____ are listening to the story.

❺ The story is about a _____ .

3

Many years ago, there was a student.

He was not good at English. His grades were always bad, and his teacher was always angry with him.

Rewrite the sentences in the past tense.

❶ The boy is a student.

The boy was a student.

❷ He is nine years old.

_____

❸ The student is not happy.

_____

❹ The teacher is angry with the boy.

_____

❺ The student's grades are bad.

_____

❻ The students study English together.

_____

The student was walking home. He was
not very happy.

"Where are you going?" asked an
old man.

"I am going home," said the boy.

"Why are you sad, my boy?"

"I am sad because my English is so bad."

What were they doing yesterday afternoon? Connect.

The boy was
walking home.

The old man was
sitting down at home.

The teacher was
writing on the board.

The girls were
doing their homework.

The girl was
reading a book.

The boys were
playing cards.

❶

❷

❸

❹

❺

❻

"My teacher is always angry with me because my English grades are usually very bad," said the boy. "I don't know how to improve my English."

"I can help you, my boy," said the old man.

Complete. Use these words:

never   sometimes   usually   always

❶ Lee Ming _sometimes_ tells stories.

❷ The boy was _____ happy in his English class.

❸ The teacher was _____ angry with the boy.

❹ The boy's English grades were _____ very bad.

How about you?

❺ My English grades are _____ very good.

❻ I _____ help my mother.

❼ I _____ ride a bicycle.

❽ I _____ do my homework.

❾ I am _____ sad.

❿ I _____ speak English at school.

"What do I have to do?" asked the boy.

"You have to bring me three hairs from a tiger."

"How can I do this? The tiger will kill me."

"You have to find a way," said the old man.

1 Connect.

❶ Students • — • has to fight fires.

• have to go to school.

❷ Doctors • • has to drive a bus.

❸ A firefighter • • have to help sick people.

❹ A teacher • • have to do your homework.

❺ We •

❻ A bus driver • • has to grade students' tests.

❼ You • • have to keep our classroom clean.

2 Complete these sentences about yourself.

❶ I have to _____.

❷ I don't have to _____.

❸ I have to _____.

❹ I don't have to _____.

"What did he do, Grandpa?"

"Where did he find a tiger, Grandpa?"

"Did the tiger kill him, Grandpa?"

"Did he kill the tiger, Grandpa?"

"All right, all right! I'm going to tell you."

Rearrange the words.

❶ he what do did ?

What did he do?

❷ see he did who ?

_____

❸ he did find the tiger where ?

_____

❹ tiger find how did he the ?

_____

❺ go the boy did home ?

_____

❻ he find did tiger's the cave ?

_____

❼ him the tiger did kill?

_____

❽ tell I'm to going you .

_____

The boy went up into the mountains.
He came to a tiger's cave. He looked
inside. The tiger was big and very hungry.
It roared loudly, so the boy ran away.

Put the sentences in order.
Number them 1 to 6.

☐ He looked inside the cave.

☐ He went into the mountains.

☐ The boy ran away.

1 The boy went to look for a tiger.

☐ He saw a big hungry tiger. It roared loudly.

☐ He saw a cave in the mountains.

That afternoon the boy came back with some food for the tiger. He put it outside the cave and walked away. The tiger roared and came out to eat the food.

1 **Copy the text on page 16.**

---

2 **Check your work. Circle Yes or No .**

❶ Did you use three capital letters?   Yes   No

❷ Did you use three periods at the end of the sentences?   Yes   No

❸ Did you leave spaces between the words?   Yes   No

❹ Did you check your spelling?   Yes   No

The next day the tiger was hungry and thirsty, so the boy gave it food to eat and water to drink. This time the boy did not walk away.

1 **Connect the present to the past.**

is   walk   give   eat   drink

gave   was   ate   drank   walked

2 **Circle the mistake and rewrite the sentence.**

❶ The tiger was (small.)

The tiger was big.

❷ The tiger was not hungry.

_____

❸ The boy gave it food to drink.

_____

❹ The tiger ate the water.

_____

❺ The boy walked away.

_____

The boy went to feed the tiger every day.
The tiger ate the food and drank the
water. It did not roar at the boy. It was
not angry.

1 Answer the questions.

❶ Did the boy feed the tiger every day?

Yes, he did.

❷ What did the tiger eat?

❸ What did the tiger drink?

❹ Did the tiger roar at the boy?

❺ Was the tiger angry?

2 Write the opposites to these words. Find them in the story.

down _up_   bad

easy   happy

never   young

small   inside

One day, the boy went to feed the tiger.
The tiger was not happy because it was
hurt. The boy saw a thorn in its foot. He
helped the tiger and pulled the thorn out.

Circle the correct words.

❶ The old man (**is**) / **was** telling the story.

❷ The children **are** / **is** listening to the story.

❸ The boy **looks** / **looked** inside a tiger's cave.

❹ The tiger **is** / **was** hungry.

❺ The boy **went** / **go** to **fed** / **feed** the tiger.

❻ The tiger **were** / **was** hurt and **unhappy** / **angry** .

❼ The boy **looks** / **looked** at the tiger's foot.

❽ There **was** / **were** a thorn **in** / **on** its foot.

❾ The boy **helped** / **was helping** the tiger.

The next day, the boy went to feed the tiger again. This time the tiger ate from the boy's hand.

As the tiger was eating, the boy pulled three hairs from its back.

Connect the words in the maze and tell the story.

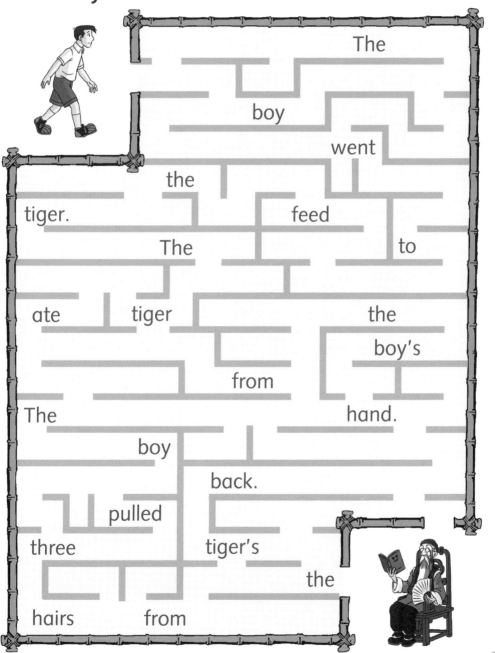

The
boy
went
the
tiger.
feed
The
to
ate
tiger
the
boy's
from
The
hand.
boy
back.
pulled
three
tiger's
the
hairs
from

The tiger was not angry. The boy said,
"Thank you," and he ran home.

He showed the three hairs to the
old man.

"What do I have to do with them,
now?" asked the boy.

Rewrite the sentences in the past tense.

➊ The tiger is angry.

   The tiger was angry.

➋ The boy is not afraid.

   _____

➌ The boy gives the tiger food and water.

   _____

➍ The tiger eats the food.

   _____

➎ The tiger drinks the water.

   _____

➏ There is a thorn in the tiger's foot.

   _____

➐ The boy helps the tiger.

   _____

➑ The boy runs home.

   _____

"How did you get those tiger hairs?" asked the old man.

"I made friends with the tiger, little by little, step by step," said the boy.

"That is how you must learn English, little by little, step by step."

Answer the questions.

1 Did the boy live in China?

Yes, he did.

2 Was he a student?

3 Were his English grades good?

4 Was his teacher happy with him?

5 Was it easy to get the tiger's hairs?

6 Did the old man help the boy?

7 Did the boy need the hairs to learn English?

"Who was that little boy, Grandpa?"
"Did you know him, Grandpa?"
"Was he your friend, Grandpa?"
"I am that little boy. After that I was good at English, and I was a happy student."

Complete the report about this book.

Book Report

Title: _____

Author: _____

Illustrator: _____

Publisher: _____

Number of pages: _____

This story is about _____

_____

New words I learned in this book

_____ _____

_____ _____

_____ _____

I think this story is...

☐ ☆☆☆☆☆ interesting

☐ ☆☆☆☆ good

☐ ☆☆☆ not bad

☐ ☆☆ OK

☐ ☆ boring

Picture Dictionary

bus driver

feed

cards

fire

cave

firefighter

doctor

food

hair

thorn

mountain

tiger

roar

water

Dolphin Readers

Dolphin Readers are available at five levels, from Starter to 4.

The Dolphins series covers four major themes:

Grammar, Living Together, The World Around Us, Science and Nature.

For each theme, there are two titles at every level.

Activity Books are available for all Dolphins.

All Dolphins are available on audio CD.
(2 TITLES ON EACH CD 💿 SEE TABLE BELOW)

Teacher's Notes are available at **www.oup.com/elt/dolphins**

	Grammar	Living Together	The World Around Us	Science and Nature
Starter	• Silly Squirrel • Monkeying Around	• My Family • A Day with Baby	• Doctor, Doctor • Moving House	• A Game of Shapes • Baby Animals
Level 1	• Meet Molly • Where Is It?	• Little Helpers • Jack the Hero	• On Safari • Lost Kitten	• Number Magic • How's the Weather?
Level 2	• Double Trouble • Super Sam	• Candy for Breakfast • Lost!	• A Visit to the City • Matt's Mistake	• Numbers, Numbers Everywhere • Circles and Squares
Level 3	• Students in Space • What Did You Do Yesterday?	• New Girl in School • Uncle Jerry's Great Idea	• Just Like Mine • Wonderful Wild Animals	• Things That Fly • Let's Go to the Rainforest
Level 4	• The Tough Task • Yesterday, Today, and Tomorrow	• We Won the Cup • Up and Down	• Where People Live • City Girl, Country Boy	• In the Ocean • Go, Gorillas, Go